Just Because I Can

encouragements, thoughts, and reflections from a local pastor

Rev. Howard D. Courtney

ISBN 978-1-990485-36-7.

Just because I can : encouragements, thoughts, and reflections from a local pastor / by Rev. Howard D. Courtney

Names: Norman Howard Dinnick Courtney, 1951–, author.
Caleb Howard Courtney, 1980–, editor.

Description: Sarnia, ON: Caleb Howard Courtney, 2022 (publisher).
Originally published by the author as a series of internet videos.

Identifiers: ISBN 978-1-990485-36-7 (paperback)
ISBN 978-1-990485-37-4 (e-book)

Subjects: Practical theology — Practical religion.
The Christian life — Works of consolation and cheer — General works — 2001–.
The Christian life — Anecdotes, etc.
The Christian life — Works of meditation and devotion — Devotional works of individual authors —Other works — By language — English — 2001–.

Classification: BV4832.3 C68 2022
BV4517 C68 2022
BV4905.3 C68 2022
248.4/C8357

Contents

Foreword

When Howard Courtney's son, Caleb, approached me about writing the forward for the book *Just Because I Can: encouragements, thoughts, and reflections from a local pastor*, it made me realize how fortunate I am to know Reverend Courtney and to benefit from his wisdom.

I meet a lot of people as Mayor of the Town of Innisfil, but Reverend Courtney is one of those people you remember and keep with you long after you have met him. His enthusiasm for the community in which he lives, and serves is inspiring. Howard Courtney, I feel, has made our town a better place.

I encourage you to read this book to see for yourself Reverend Courtney's impact on our community.

He does all of this, just because he can.

Lynn Dollin, Mayor
Town of Innisfil

—1—
Amazing People

https://vimeo.com/356537740

As we recently celebrated forty years of ministry here at Innisfil Community Church, I was reminiscing. I was looking through some of the photo albums of events, activities, and news items over the past years.

It's amazing to me to see how significant individuals in the church have been. There are some who joined us forty years ago and who are still with us. As we look across the faces in those photographs, it's amazing to consider how many of the individuals have gone around the world, many of them sharing Jesus in full time ministry, and others simply moving on to other places and other churches.

I'm so glad that we have people from our church represented all over the world—people who love Jesus and have been impacted by this church.

Thank you! Thank you for being part of that.

We continue to impact kids every day of the week here through Innisfil Community Church.

I thought I'd share this with you just because I can.

—2—
Prayer Works!

https://vimeo.com/357881815

Well again, I have been thinking and looking over the past. I was reflecting on how a few years ago, Innisfil Community Church was going through financial difficulties and challenges. There were times where we couldn't even make our mortgage principal payments. It was a stressful time.

During that time, one of our board members who had been coming into the church regularly in the early morning hours to pray said, "I think we should implement a church board prayer meeting." That's exactly what we did. We started a prayer meeting every Tuesday and Thursday morning from 7:00 to 8:00 every morning. We implemented a prayer meeting on Sunday mornings from 7:30 to 8:30.

We began to pray, and wouldn't you know it? Things have turned around. God has blessed us. Our financial stresses have decreased significantly. We're now in a bit of a place of comfort financially. We're rejoicing in God! Who knows what happens when people pray?

I share this with you today just because I can.

—3—
Toothpaste

https://vimeo.com/356538511

Here I am again, pondering on life. My mind goes to weird places at times. I was thinking of toothpaste. Particularly, this brand of toothpaste called Aquafresh.

It has three different colours of stripes in one package. I wondered how those three stripes end up coming out of this single tube? When I squeeze it, it comes out in stripes! Most people have never stopped to think how this happens, nor do they understand it. Some people think that if you cut the tube open there will be three separate compartments. But really, it's not! It's still all one compartment, and there's a science behind it called rheology. It has to do with the density of the paste. The pressure on the ingredients is applied consistently, which maintains the three stripes.

As I think about this, I wonder why is it that we have to understand God before we trust him? We can't even understand rheology—how toothpaste can come out of a tube in three stripes and yet still be one unit. Why do we have to understand God to trust him? There are so many other things we don't understand, and that we just believe and trust.

So today, when you're going about your normal duties and routines of life, don't think you need to have God figured out in order to trust him. Put your trust and faith in him even when you don't understand him, and he will be there to help you through your journey.

I share that with you—just a few thoughts—because I can.

—4—
The Single Most Important Thing

https://vimeo.com/356547962

Well I'm down at the lake again, pondering on the things of God. I was thinking, "What single thing is there that makes the difference in a Christian's life? What is it that keeps a person strong? What is it that feeds their faith?" In all my years of ministry, and looking over the last forty years at Innisfil Community Church, I think the one most significant thing in life in serving Jesus is to have a regular daily devotion. There's seldom a day that would go by where I do not read the scriptures and take time to meditate on them, and I think that's the key for every Christian. I have never met a

Christian who has backslidden or lost their faith, that I know of, who has had a consistent daily devotion. It's sort of like eating every day! You need to feed yourself in order to live and in order to survive. It's the same with our faith. If we don't feed our faith, we won't maintain it. Get into the Bible, even if you only read a small portion every day. Read it and meditate on it.

I share this with you, as a secret of faith, just because I can!

—5—
Days of Harvest

https://vimeo.com/356528362

I'm out here in a hay field, and it reminds me of my teenage years, when I was growing up with my best friend Philip. We were cousins, and he lived on a farm. Every once in a while—not often, but occasionally—I would end up on the farm with him in the haying season. This was the time when we were bailing hay and bringing the harvest in.

Growing up at that time was also significant in the life of the church because there was a real harvest mentality in the church. The church believed that Jesus was coming soon, and that we had a job to do to bring in the harvest. In fact, if the harvest wasn't brought in on time, it would actually be lost!

That mentality has served me well over the years. I still believe as strongly as ever that Jesus is coming soon, and that we have a job to bring in the harvest. We need labourers. The Bible says, "Pray that the Lord of the harvest would send forth labourers into the harvest field." We need labourers these days to bring people to Jesus.

I'm so glad I have that passion in my heart. It was embedded within me as a young child growing up, and I hope you catch a little bit of that passion to bring people to Jesus.

I share this with you today just because I can!

—6—
Life's Detours

https://vimeo.com/356527137

Detours. None of us really invite them into our lives. They just come unexpectedly. There are a lot of people who experienced detours in the scriptures. Joseph had many detours in his life. David experienced a lot of detours in his life as well. And we experience them! They come unexpectedly. All of a sudden, we find ourselves heading down a road we hadn't planned on.

But let's pause for a moment. M`ost of those detours are there to help us get to our destination better. God sometimes takes us down those detour roads because he knows there's devastation on the road we're going down. So he blocks the road and puts up a sign, indicating that road isn't the best way for you to go.

So, if you're in the midst of a detour right now in your life, interrupted in the path that you were planning, trust God! Honour him! Go on his path! He's got the ultimate destiny planned for you—one that is the very best for you. It's a great plan, and by following his detours you'll arrive safely.

It's something to think about! I share this with you just because I can.

—7—
Seedlings

https://vimeo.com/358954999

Sowing seeds. Forty years ago, a small group of us gathered together with plans for our church property. After a visit from the local conservation authorities in Midhurst, Ontario, we were able to secure several hundreds of little seedlings. We came to this property, that had then just been purchased, and we began to plant seedlings.

Forty years later, as you can see behind me, there is now a hedge that is far greater and far bigger than I am. It is far taller and far more beautiful than I am. This hedge has been established because of those seeds that were planted forty years ago.

Now, probably dozens of those trees never did spring forth and grow, but these are some of the ones that did. When I look back over the forty years of ministry here at Innisfil Community Church, we recognize that there are many seeds that we've sown that have never produced fruit. But we're so thankful that not all the seed went to waste. Many people made commitments to Christ, many people were healed, many people were delivered, many people received what they needed, families were strengthened, and God's kingdom grew. We're so thankful that we began planting seeds many years ago.

I'm just thinking about that and wondering, "What kind of seeds are we planting now that will bring forth fruit forty years from today?" What are you planting? What are the seedlings in your hands? Are you expecting and believing God for a fruitful reward of your investment?

I share this with you today just because I can.

—8—
After 40 Years . . . Now What?

https://vimeo.com/358956438

The number forty has many references in the Bible. In the account of the great flood with Noah, it rained 40 days and 40 nights. We don't want to go there! When Jesus prepared for his public ministry, he was tempted for forty days in the wilderness. We don't really want to go there either! Israel spent forty years wandering in the wilderness with Moses. We really don't want to go there!

As a church, we have been in ministry for forty years here at Innisfil Community Church. We're now looking towards what happens after forty years. We're trusting God that this is going to be a breakthrough year as we enter another decade of ministry. Forty years has passed, but we're moving forward.

There's so much more to be done, and we're so glad that we're part of a church family that is much bigger than just us. We're a part of the Pentecostal Assemblies of Canada, a worldwide missions organization, and we believe there are many people yet to find Christ as Saviour. We're going to work towards that and believe God for it, and we're believing God for it right here in Innisfil.

Will you join with us and pray that God will give us a great harvest as we move forward in this new decade to come?

God bless you, and thank you!

I share this with you just because I can.

—9—
Feeling Empty or Forsaken?

https://vimeo.com/361391958

In recent years, a lot of people have become very intrigued with old vacated buildings like this one. The interesting thing about this building is that although it still exists, it really doesn't house anybody. It's empty! There's nothing inside except the empty remains of what once was a place where someone lived.

I was thinking about this, and I thought about how often we can feel like there's nothing left in us. We're empty. We're of no use. We've been left abandoned.

As I thought about that, I thought how there are many people who are actually watching us when we feel abandoned, when we feel useless, and when we feel like we're of no use to anybody. These people are standing back in admiration, just like I am admiring this old house today. Looking at the remains, there's something beautiful about it. There's something about the memories there. There's something about it that adds to our lives, just by observing it. It's intriguing! I find it very neat to be able to stop by and take a peek in some of these spots.

Well, if you're feeling lonely, forsaken, or empty today, just remember that somebody's watching you, and they see a lot more in you than you might see in yourself today.

I share this with you just because I can.

—10—
The Wishing Well

https://vimeo.com/361391420

I'm sitting here on the edge of a well. This well has been around for a long time. The early Europeans began to believe that wells were special and held some sort of magical powers. They developed a system where they would throw coins in the well, and the well would become known as a wishing well. As they threw coins into the well, they had some sort of wish they hoped and believed would come true because of the magical powers and deities that provided life in the well.

A long time ago, there was a man named Jesus who met a woman at a well. It was there he disclosed to her many of the things in her life that she could hardly believe that he knew about. It was there that he offered life itself to her.

If you are depending on some kind of special wish to come true, and throwing money into a well to make it so, you need to discover this: it's not the well, or even the water in the well, that brings life. It was he who came to the well—Jesus—who offered life abundantly. It's much better to put your trust and faith in him, than just to believe by throwing some coin into a wishing well that your wish might become true.

I encourage you today to put your trust in Jesus. He is able to bring every promise true.

I share this with you just because I can!

—11—
Heritage Home

https://vimeo.com/364061255

I'm standing in front of a home that is currently being moved. This home is now on stilts and on a new foundation, preparing to be moved onto a new foundation. When most people drive by this location, they simply see another home. But this is more than just another old home. This home has been designated as a heritage home in our town. This is the Wauchope Home. There's been a lot of discussion about it, and a lot of debate in our community about it, wondering why it's not already placed on a new foundation.

The developer behind us is developing a whole new subdivision and it had to be moved to make room for it. Part of the agreement is that this home must be preserved because in our town we're concerned about our heritage, and some of the history and the roots we have in our municipality.

As I began to think about that, I thought about our Christian faith. I wonder if you take time to really think about your roots, your heritage of faith, your foundation. Sometimes the foundations have to change. Sometimes we have to go back and do it over again.

So I'm wondering about your faith. Do you recognize that probably your parents or grandparents were praying for you for years? They may have been praying about this very day in your life. Maybe it's time to take a look back to your history, to go back to your roots, and get re-established in the faith, trusting Jesus Christ. Looking into the Bible and rediscovering the foundations that we have.

I share this with you today just because I can.

—12—
Canadian "Tire"

https://vimeo.com/364061000

Here we are at the Canadian Tire store. It's an interesting store. It's been around for a long time in our country. What most people don't realize though, is that although it started as a tire store, it is no longer simply a tire store. In fact it's predominantly not a tire store anymore. Through these doors you'll find all kinds of other things.

When I started thinking about that, I thought of Christianity. A lot of people think Christianity is simply a group of rules—of do's and don'ts—but they've never entered the door to discover that there's so much more! Once you enter the door of Christianity, it's full of treasures all over. It's more than just a list of rules, more than just an institution—

it's about a relationship with Jesus Christ. It's so important that we open the door to discover what's really inside.

If' you're searching out faith, put your faith in Jesus Christ, and open the door to discover some of the great truths that are there for you.

I share this with you today just because I can. Because Canadian Tire is about more than just tires!

—13—
The Master Creator/Artist

https://vimeo.com/367567573

What an awesome part of God's creation! In only a few seconds you can look into the water falls, see the beauty of God's creation; look to the sky and see the formations of the clouds; actually look into the trees and see the colours as they change; the rocks as they fall alongside of the waterfalls.

When you begin to look at this and see the masterful work of an artist, constantly painting new pictures every second, how can you imagine a God like that who does not care for you? In fact, he's the God who sees you as more vital and more significant and more important than any other part of his creation., Understanding this masterful creator, how can you go away not recognizing your significance in this world. God has created you uniquely and beautifully to have an impact on this world.

I trust that as you look at this picture and see the greatness of God's creation, that you begin to realize how significant you are to him.

Have a wonderful and blessed day. I share this with you today just because I can!

—14—
I See Red

https://vimeo.com/369072165

I see red! Isn't it gorgeous? The leaves, as they have changed this season, have been so brilliant and wonderful. I'm amazed at the brilliance of the red.

The colour red is rather interesting because when people say, "I see red," they often think of anger. They are seeing red because of anger. Well, if that's what happens to you, then you need to enroll in an anger management course that will help you tame your anger and control it! It will help you realize that no one can make you mad.

But there's another red that is really significant in terms of our Christian faith. I'm thinking of when Jesus Christ went to the cross and died on the cross for us. He shed his precious blood to be the sacrifice for our sins. It's blood red. Blood red is that colour that describes what Jesus has done for us.

For all of those who come to Jesus and ask for forgiveness, the Bible says his blood cleanses us from all sin. Now, if you haven't done that already, I encourage you to do that. Just bow to him in prayer, and say, "God, forgive me of my sin. Let your blood wash me clean, and I'll be forever thankful and grateful to you!"

I share this with you today just because I can!

—15—
Roof Maintenance

https://vimeo.com/369486113

This is a very large roof! It's the roof on our newest building at Innisfil Community Church. We built this ten years ago, and we expected these shingles to last us for twenty-five years. It's only ten years in, and they're really dilapidated and showing signs of deterioration, and are in some places very insecure. So, we've decided to go ahead and do some maintenance. The stripping along the bottom is preparation for a steel roof that is about to be installed.

It's sort of like life. Life needs maintenance. If we don't care for it now, it's going to cost us greatly in the future. Your family, your home, your marriage, your spiritual life—all of those need maintenance too. The question is, will you get to it soon enough where you don't have to invest an entire lifetime trying to fix it? The sooner you get to it, the easier it will be to repair it.

So I encourage you today to take a look at what maintenance needs to be done in your family, in your marriage, and in your spiritual life. Get to it quickly!

I share this with you today just because I can.

—16—
The Honey House

https://vimeo.com/371934800

I'm at the honey house. Dickie Bee Honey. It's a local market place where you can buy just about anything you want from bee products. It's a sweet place! If you are in the area of Innisfil, it's a place that's worth dropping by.

It's here that I'm reminded of a saying that "You can catch more flies with honey than you can with vinegar." We all know what the saying means—it means that you can accomplish a lot more by being friendly rather than having a caustic attitude.

There are some people that have caustic attitudes! But you don't want to be one of those! You want to be someone who is making a difference in the community and making a difference in the lives of other people.

I challenge you today, check your attitude. Do you find yourself feeling disjointed, out of place, and not a happy person? Maybe you need to change your attitude and discover that "honey attracts more flies than vinegar." You can have a lot more relationships, and your relationships can be much better, by making sure you have a good attitude. Share yourself with other people in meaningful and productive ways. You can do it! It's worth it!

I share this with you today just because I can!

—17—
Brrrrr . . . It's Cold Out Here!

https://vimeo.com/373445266

Brrrrr . . . it's cold out here! When that snow and cold weather comes so suddenly and we're not expecting it, our whole body sure feels it! It seems so much better when it comes gradually, and you can get adapted to it and you don't notice it so much. But when it swarms in like it has recently, it's just plain cold!

In thinking about this from a spiritual perspective, I think there are two different things that could happen to you in your life of faith. You could either "go cold" in your faith or "grow cold" in your faith. For some people, faith *goes* cold. This could be because of difficulties or experiences—maybe a death in the in the family, or maybe a sudden unexpected death, or maybe a divorce, or some major tragedy. Our faith can suddenly go cold. We reject faith and step back from it.

Then there is the other possibility. Over time, people don't realize it, but they don't feed their faith, they don't nurture their faith, and they simply *grow* cold.

In essence, at the end of the day, both scenarios are *cold*. They're missing something significant. They need the fire of God once again.

But I've got good news for you! You can fan the flames. I could start a bonfire here and feel the warmth of that flame, and you can do the same in your spiritual journey. Light a fire underneath you. Get back to reading the scriptures. Take time to pray. It's amazing what can happen! You can move on, renew faith, and get warmed up again.

I share this with you today just because I can!

—18—
Piggyback

https://vimeo.com/375226914

I've got a new friend today, and he's quite a character. He's really helping me a lot! He seems to be carrying me. Remember those days of piggybacking? You had to trust the person that was carrying you, because they might not be able to hold on to you.

When someone else is carrying you piggyback, it's a lot of fun and you don't have to do the work. The problem is, we can't do that all the time. Sometimes we've got to be the guy below doing the carrying. It's only fair.

So in this life, if you're just counting on everybody else carrying you, look up. There's a better way. It's okay for others to carry you through a hard time, but not always. You ought to be turning it around and saying, "How can I help you? How can I help take the weight off your shoulders? Why don't you jump on mine, and I'll carry you for a little while? Let me share the burden."

Isn't that what spiritual life is all about? We surrender our lives to Jesus Christ, and he actually carries us through life. We have to trust him completely. 100%. Always.

It's worth thinking about. I share this with you today just because I can!

—19—
Just Thankful

https://vimeo.com/376035696

They say a picture paints a thousand words. There are couple of pictures here. The manger scene is a picture of the wonderful gift of God. He loves us so much that he sends his son, Jesus, to be born, and lays him to rest in a manger, coming to save us. A saviour to us is born.

Then there is a second picture that moves from the manger scene to the cross. The cross is that symbol of the crucifixion, the time of horrible pain and suffering for Jesus as he gave his life for us. This is another wonderful gift given for you and me.

As I think of these symbols, they hold meaning at any time of the year for us—Christmas, Easter, and maybe even Thanksgiving. Today, I'm just very thankful for these gifts. The gift of Jesus as a babe in the manger, and the gift of Jesus on the cross, dying for my sins. What a wonderful gift. It's worth taking time to think about. It's a great time to be thankful and grateful.

I share this with you today, just because I can.

—20—
Putting Idle Hands to Work

https://vimeo.com/378110719

We live in a rural community with lots of villages and hamlets around us. The total population of the town of Innisfil, Ontario, is about 35,000 people. In our town, we've got a lot of kids and youth. I see some of them hanging out at Tim Hortons, the local coffee shop, with no place to go and no activities for them to do.

Some people thought we should be doing something more for them. This space I'm standing in is a part of Innisfil Community Church. It's about 800 square feet, and we decided this space could be used by the community as a youth drop-in centre. This is an opportunity to provide for the kids in the community. They can come here to participate in any number of activities.

There's a Bible verse that says, "Idle hands are the devil's tools." We are endeavouring to provide a space where kids can hang out, do homework, or play games. This is a great opportunity for us, and for these kids. This is what a church is meant to be. A place where we can provide services for the community, and help to provide strength where there is lack around us. We're looking forward to the development of this space to become that kind of a place for our youth in the community.

I don't know about you, but if you've got idle hands, you ought to find some way to put them to use to make this world a better place. God's put you here with purpose. Find your purpose. Get involved. Support what's happening that's great in the community, and God will use you in ways that you would never have dreamed of.

We're hoping that this space will be one of those kinds of spaces.

I share this with you today just because I can!

—21— Who Gets the Credit?

https://vimeo.com/379520808

It's Christmas time, and there's so much excitement in our community! Behind me, there are seventy-five boxes. These boxes were made available because of the generosity of people in the community. Some people gave us funds so that we could buy the boxes. They were purchased at cost from Innisfil Self Storage, and we're thankful for their contribution. The boxes were wrapped by the Innisfil Rotary Club, and they've provided the paper and supplies and made a work bee to make the boxes as they are.

Each of these boxes contains the ingredients for a full course turkey dinner. Everything needed to make a turkey dinner is in each of these seventy-five boxes. Foodland, a grocery store in Stroud, so generously donated fifty ten-pound bags of potatoes to go in these boxes. Then, Innisfil Fire and Rescue Station No. 2 in Stroud has been so kind to donate seventy-five turkeys, ready to be put in the boxes as they are packed. These boxes are now ready for seventy-five families to have a full Christmas dinner.

My thought today is that it is amazing what can be done if you don't care who gets the credit! Let me say it again. It's amazing what you can accomplish if you don't care who gets the credit. So many people contributing in so many ways can make a huge difference. The next time you decide to give, don't worry about who gets the credit. Just know that you are giving to the most vulnerable people in the community, and that you are doing it because it's the right thing to do.

We are so thankful to be a part of such a great community.

I share this with you today just because I can.

—22—
Traffic Circles

https://vimeo.com/380945543

Traffic circles really aren't new, but in our town, our first traffic circle has been constructed on the Sixth Line of Innisfil. As you go around, you recognize that the traffic circle provides certain exits along the way. This one isn't really open yet, so the exits aren't fully available. I discovered that in this traffic circle, you can go around and around and around almost forever and really find yourself getting nowhere! First, you need to know your destination, and second, you need to know which exit to take to get there.

It's sort of like life. If you don't know where you're going, and you don't know where the exits are to take you there, you might be on a circle spinning forever. It's so important to know where you are, and where you want to go, and to make the right exits.

Sometimes we get so busy in life that we don't take time to realize that we're just going in circles, and we're not getting to where we need to go. I want to challenge you with these thoughts today. If you're on a traffic circle, going nowhere in life, take a moment and pull off to the side. Evaluate where you are, and where you want to go, and what exit will take you there. It will make a world of difference for you.

I share this with you just because I can!

—23—
Communications

https://vimeo.com/381840029

I'm standing at the base of a local communications tower. You will see these spread throughout every one of our communities. It's amazing when you begin to realize how many people are impacted by this one single tower. I don't have a number, but I know thousands and thousands of calls are made through this tower every hour of every day. It's an amazing network.

We have been given the knowledge and ability to create these things. Communication is so significant in our day and age. Who would have ever thought that everybody would be walking down the street with a device that's connected and interconnected with family and friends and people around the world? It's amazing!

As I think about that structure, my mind goes to the spirit realm. God, in his creative ability, established what we call "prayer"—communication between any individual on the planet directly with him. Conversations can take place spontaneously with God, no matter where we are. Such a valuable tool we have! I wonder how often we use the tool of prayer to communicate with the creator, God, who loves you and cares for you, and has your best interest in mind.

Communication. Just thinking about it. I'm sharing this with you just because I can!

—24—
Running To and Fro

https://vimeo.com/382896241

It was years ago when I first read a scripture talking about people "running to and fro" in the last days. You don't have to look very far to discover that this is sort of what happens every day in our society. Just take a walk in the mall, and there are hundreds of people walking almost every day in the mall. If you are looking for signs of the end times, you don't need to go far.

The question is, are you running with purpose? Do you have a purpose for where you are going? At the end of the day, do you know what you are trying to accomplish? Setting your priorities, understanding where you're going, and why you're going there, will make a huge difference in your life. Take time today to consider, "Why am I investing my time running to and fro? Does it have a purpose, or am I just going around in circles?"

Just some thoughts about the last days, running to and fro. I hope you've got a purpose. I hope you know where you're going, and I hope your destiny is fixed on heaven.

Have a good day! I share this with you today just because I can.

—25—
Feeling Hollow?

https://vimeo.com/384290493

Some trees are so strong on the outside, but inside they're just hollow! Interesting story. People's lives are sometimes like that as well. They look great on the outside where everything seems to be wonderful, but inside there's a hollowness that nobody seems to see.

I've got news for you—there's something that can happen to you that can change your life around! You can invite Jesus Christ into your heart and into your life to live within you and bring life to you! He'll bring strength to you so that the inside can look as great as the outside.

Just a few thoughts I will leave with you today! Have a great day! I share these thoughts with you today just because I can.

—26—
Snow Days and Snow Storms

https://vimeo.com/385710968

Who loves a storm like me? I love it once in a while when a major storm shuts everything down and nobody can move to go anywhere. All of a sudden, everything stops. As a kid I used to love that. I would walk out in the streets knowing there would be no cars going by. We've still got a few cars going by here today because this highway, Highway 11, is a major road through our town of Innisfil, Ontario.

I wonder why it is that we don't stop once in a while to "smell the roses"—to appreciate those things we usually take for granted. I remember the biblical mandate of the sabbath, to have one day of rest among the seven. It might do us good sometimes to realize that the world doesn't revolve around us. Sometimes, after a good snowstorm, when everything stops, we really haven't gotten behind at all, but may actually find ourselves further ahead! We're better rested, refreshed, and probably get to live longer because we've looked after ourselves and taken a break.

I don't know where you're at and what's happening in your life, but maybe a good snow day would be helpful to get you back on track. Maybe it would even help you to realize that there's something more important than just running a massive rat-race, day in, day out, seven days a week. Take a day off. Hey, maybe even consider going to church. Why don't you try something different and unique? Join us in church Sunday. We'd love to see you there!

I share this with you today just because I can!

—27—
Are You Building Bridges or Barriers?

https://vimeo.com/385710503

One of the bridges behind me was built to transport people under the Highway 400, a major highway that runs through our community, so that they might get from one side of the highway to the other. This bridge has allowed that to happen for years.

Over the years, traffic has increased, the community has grown, and now we need a larger road to transport people across the 400 Highway. This one will transport people over the highway. So, the province of Ontario is building a new bridge. It's a huge bridge! It's just a humongous stretch of a bridge going over the highway, especially in our community! I think the province is doing some things right when it comes to building bridges.

When we begin to consider some of these things, we might consider a parallel within our own lives. What are we building? We're really good at building barriers, but how significant it is for us to build bridges to help people to get where they are going. As individuals we will always run into barriers. Life is filled with barriers. But how wonderful it is when someone comes along and builds a bridge where there was a barrier for you before.

I invite you today to start being intentional about building bridges to help other people get to where they are going. You can do it. It can make a huge difference in other peoples lives. It will actually help you in the end as well.

Just a thought! I share this with you today just because I can.

—28— Entrapped

https://vimeo.com/385709988

I think I can safely say that none of us ever want to be involved in a motor vehicle accident, much less become trapped in our vehicles because of one. In the case of the scene behind me, the people involved in this collision are waiting for extrication. The emergency responders will be arriving soon to do the extrication, and the individuals, who are not injured, are waiting to be removed from their vehicles.

I wonder how many times that accidents like this happen in the spiritual realm, where we find ourselves entrapped where we never expected to be. We might be trapped by all kinds of habits, situations that are seemingly beyond our control. We need somebody else bigger than us, and more equipped than us, to come and set us free.

Isn't that exactly what God has done for us? He's made a way for us to find help, find deliverance, and to find a way out. Don't remain captive, stuck in your situation, when there is help available. The people behind me called 911. Maybe you need to simply call on God and ask him for his help and receive the help he provides along the way.

Again, I'm sharing my thoughts with you today just because I can!

—29—
Let Problems Melt Away

https://vimeo.com/390215231

We've all had dreams as kids to build a snowman. The snowman beside me is not your typical snowman—it is huge! It's gigantic! It's not far from our home in Innisfil, Ontario.

When you think of this snowman, it's like some of the stuff in our lives. We've created situations much larger than us. Sometimes these can be a joy, other times they can be obstacles. When these things become obstacles in your way, there are a few ways that we can deal with them. First, you can deliberately change the atmosphere around you, and all of a sudden, they will melt and disappear. Or, you can actually leave them alone, let them go, and sooner or later, the environment changes around us, a new season comes, and they will melt and disappear naturally over time.

Problems in our life are sometimes like this. There are some times we have to bring out a "heater" and apply it to our situation to make it dissipate and go away. Other times it's better just to leave alone until the environment changes around it.

I don't know what you're facing in life, or what obstacle stands in your way. Maybe it began as a pleasure but now it's an obstacle. You can allow it to continue, or you can take some action and make a difference, causing it to dissipate. Or maybe it's one of those things that if you irritate it, it just gets larger, colder, and you create a more frozen or frigid state, worse than before. Decide what you have to do, and then let your problems be addressed accordingly.

I'm just thinking about this, and thought I'd share it with you just because I can!

—30—
Light a Candle

https://vimeo.com/391724952

Ouch! What just hit me in the head? It's dark in here! I guess that's a lesson for us today. Why is it so often that people curse the darkness instead of lighting a candle? I discovered this saying long ago: "It's more important to light a candle than to curse the darkness."

I find that in our society there are too many people around that are cursing the darkness instead of lighting a candle. You see, when you light a candle, you bring hope. You bring light in the midst of darkness. You change circumstances for the better. We have a choice to do this. We have a choice to come alongside someone who is discouraged, sad, dejected, or feeling bad. Light a candle! Help them take their next steps forward to happiness and joy once again!

I like the saying, “It’s better to light a candle instead of cursing the darkness.”

I share it with you today just because I can!

—31— Always There

https://vimeo.com/393218596

I am standing by a piece of equipment that many people might have in their homes. It's a furnace. Yours may be different than this–electric, or some other form of heat—but this one is a gas-powered furnace. It provides heat for our home.

I don't spend a lot of time down here looking at it. I don't compliment it, or tell it how well it works. I don't tell it how much I appreciate it. In fact, I sometimes neglect it, and even forget to change the air filter on it.

I started thinking about this, and thought how that's sometimes how we treat our family. We don't always communicate with them. We don't talk with them. We don't acknowledge them. We don't spend time with them. How neglectful we are in these areas at times!

Even worse than this, we can often neglect our relationship with God. Oh, we know he's there. He's there when we need him. But do we take time to really spend time acknowledging him, thanking him, or recognizing the good things that he does for us? In the cold nights of the soul he's there to warm our hearts and encourage us. He might even send someone to us in our times of difficulty. How often we've forgotten to say thank you, or to acknowledge him.

I'm suggesting, just as you shouldn't neglect your furnace, neither should you neglect your relationship with God. You may not regularly acknowledge him, you may not regularly communicate with him, you may not regularly thank him for his help in your life. Maybe now is the time to do these things. Maybe it's time to stop treating him like your furnace, closed up and largely ignored in a closet in some remote part of your life.

I share this thought with you today just because I can.

—32—
An Elevating Experience

https://vimeo.com/394706184

I am here today in an elevator. Why is it that for many people, their greatest fear is being trapped in an elevator? While we're moving from one floor to another, we're aiming to get to a particular destination. When we feel trapped, it sometimes overwhelms us. When we get to the correct level, we hope the elevator will stop and the door will open for us.

Sure enough, this elevator has brought us to our destination, and we can get off here if we would like. For many people who feel trapped, they wonder how they can change their circumstances. "How can I get out of this mess?"

I've pushed a button again, the door has closed, and we're moving on to the next floor. The strange thing with this, is that this second floor is a little different. Instead of the door opening on the same side that we were expecting earlier, the door actually opens in the other direction! That's correct, on the other side.

Here's the thought for today. If you're feeling trapped by circumstances—maybe by your marriage, maybe finances, or something else—take a look around. There's probably a door opening in a different direction for you! Maybe you need to change your circumstances so that you can enjoy the present better, but take a look around, because there is probably a door opening in the opposite direction for you.

I share this with you today just because I can!

—33—
Lacking Air!

https://vimeo.com/396213560

"Well, the old grey mare ain't what she used to be!" I'm not talking about me. I'm talking about an antique car that sits in my garage. It has sat here over the wintertime. During that time, I've noticed a change in this vehicle. In fact, as I walked by it, I realized that some of the air has gone out of this tire. It needs attention!

As I thought about this in terms of life, this can be something that happens to us. Sometimes we lose air! We get the wind knocked out of us sometimes! So then, we need to ask ourselves the question, "What am I going to do?" We need attention in some form. We need to care for it. Otherwise, it will cause more damage.

As I read the prophet Habakkuk in the scriptures, he told us that he was going to rejoice in God, regardless of the circumstances. God doesn't change. In difficult circumstances, I will rejoice, and I will give thanks to my God because he is going to be there for me. He's not going to leave me broken and winded. He's going to put wind back in my sails! He'll do it for you! Just take time to talk to him. He'll give you some specific instructions to help you.

I share these thoughts with you today just because I can!

—34—
Press Pause

https://vimeo.com/397717158

It's that time again where I share my thoughts with you just because I can! The T.V. behind me is turned off. It's been on a lot recently. We've been listening to what's happening around the world and in our own country with regards to the COVID-19 virus that has been spreading around the world causing widespread deaths.

When you turn the news on, it always seems to be more bad news. We're overwhelmed with it. We see all kinds of different responses to it. People are running to the store, hoarding, buying toilet paper and other items to satisfy some of the uncertainty of the future.

I don't have any great recommendation to prevent you from feeling overwhelmed, but maybe one of the first things you should do is to turn off the T.V. for a little while. Allow some space for sanity in our own lives. Watching the news has taken a toll on us. It's so negative. It's filled with anxiety and fear. A little break might do us all good.

We need to be vigilant, no question. We should not be ignorant of the things going on around us. But we also need moments where we stop, take a breath, and enjoy our lives for a few moments apart from the surrounding chaos. Try it out! You might feel a lot better at the end of the day.

I'm sharing this with you today just because I can!

—35— Surreal

https://vimeo.com/399546330

It's a strange thing to be in a huge store like this with very few customers. Most people are wearing gloves. Others are using sanitizer on their hands and wiping down the shopping carts before they use them. People are wearing masks. It's a very surreal moment to stand by and watch what's happening all around us. We just never know one day to the next what it will look like.

In these days of uncertainty there is certainly unrest, anxiety, fear, and all kinds of things happening internally. We don't really know what to do. We haven't got the resources to look beyond. We wonder what tomorrow will be like. Nevertheless, we need to hold steady. We need to be careful. We need to be vigilant. We need to do our part to ensure we don't pass on the virus to anyone else. So today, I'd just encourage you to respect "social distancing" and other protocols recommended by our local health authorities. Take the steps that are needed, and help our country to heal from this wicked virus.

I share this with you today just because I can.

—36—
"BELIEVE"

https://vimeo.com/401696294

If you live in the town of Innisfil, Ontario, I'm sure you have passed this familiar scene. One word, fastened to this particular building. "Believe." It's a word that evokes all kinds of deeper meaning. In this moment in history, the world is changing. Everything around us seems to be uncertain. It's in times like these that we really need something to believe in. Something that is greater than ourselves. Something that carries us through the difficult times.

For me, I have made a commitment of my life to Jesus Christ. I take the Bible as my source of authority in life. I have found in that, that there is security, hope, faith, and something to believe in. Take this word—"believe"—to your heart. Think about it. What do you believe in?

Maybe you should start digging deeper, and find out that there is a God who loves you and cares for you.

I share these thoughts with you today just because I can.

—37—
Watching Paint Dry

https://vimeo.com/404181667

I am in my garage painting a couple of signs. We've changed our food bank procedures, and now we have some new procedures. So I thought we need a couple of extra signs and I'm trying to prepare for some of that now.

Sitting here, I'm thinking I could sit here all night to watch the paint dry. This is what it's sort of like right now in our society and in our world. People are just sitting back, hoping that this COVID-19 virus will pass. But, as we've heard so often, unless we do our part, it won't. So make sure you are doing your "social distancing." Make sure you are not meeting in groups. Make sure you are washing your hands well and often. The more we follow these protocols, the sooner we can get back together.

I saw a post on social media of someone standing in front of their church saying, "We're going to be back soon, we just don't know when." That's so true. Someone else said, "Watching paint dry is as slow as the second coming of Christ." We know Jesus is coming back, we just don't know how soon!

We hope the virus passes so we can get back together really soon. We also anticipate the second coming of Christ, and believe that's going to happen too. We're going to do all of the things we need to do in preparation for these things, whether its for the second coming of Jesus, or the coming back together after COVID-19.

I share these few thoughts with you today just because I can. Now, back to my painting.

—38—
Easter Sunrise

https://vimeo.com/406651062

Here I am at a park along the waterfront in Belle Ewart, a little hamlet in our town of Innisfil, Ontario. It's Easter Sunday morning, Resurrection Sunday! I'm a little disappointed this morning because it is usually right here, on the lakeshore, that we gather together with a number of ministers every Easter Sunday morning sunrise to celebrate the resurrection of Jesus. My good friend and colleague, Rev. Glen Eagle, usually coordinates the service, and we stand along the shoreline and with the other ministers and Christian friends, we celebrate.

This year, I'm a little disappointed we can't gather or congregate to celebrate together. But friends, in the midst of the disappointment that we can't congregate, we can still celebrate at home in our own individual ways. It's important that we recognize that the true meaning of the resurrection of Christ. The meaning and the effect of this has not changed.

Jesus has risen! He has risen indeed! And I'm excited about the resurrection. That helps the disappointment that I can't be together with others today. We look forward to that time when we can congregate once again to gather and celebrate our faith together.

Meanwhile, stay at home and keep safe. Think and reflect on what Jesus did for us on that first great Easter sunrise.

I share this with you today just because I can.

—39—
Beauty All Around

https://vimeo.com/409553741

What an awesome place to be in Innisfil, Ontario. This is a beautiful part of God's creation. Today, I'm just outside looking over the lake across some of the properties in Innisfil, and it's gorgeous! It's a little cool. It's been raining a little bit. Most people, though, are stuck inside because of COVID-19. What a beautiful opportunity we have to pause and say thanks to God for all of his blessings to us. We have been so blessed in so many ways. Now, when everything has sort of stopped, it's a great time to say, "God, thanks for the beautiful creation we enjoy every day." So often we just miss it.

I'm sharing this with you today just because I can.

—40—
Up the Creek

https://vimeo.com/411868687

It's one of those days where we've got time. Things are shut down, and we're not supposed to be in crowds, so I've gone for a little walk in a little bit of a gulley, and I found this beautiful spot. I can see the creek flowing beautifully. The sound is amazing. I've even got some great company with my wife, Beulah, and it's just a great spot.

With everything closed down, it's a great time to take a moment to smell the roses. It's an opportunity to visit and explore nearby spots that we have never paid much attention to in the normal rush of life. Who knows what might be there in store for us! There is great beauty around us that we often miss just because we don't take the time. We get so busy.

This is such a beautiful spot. The sound of the running water is amazing. I'm sharing it with you today just because I can!

—41—
Obstacles

https://www.youtube.com/watch?v=UD5dKrQfLi0

So what happens to you when you come to a blockage on the road—in this case, a tree falling down across the pathway? Are you going to decide to climb over it? Go around it? Or maybe it's just enough to cause you to turn around and go back instead? Well, that's what's happening on this pathway we're visiting. Walking today, we're going to go over it and we're going to keep on going and to see what we can see on the other side. We're doing a little exploring of nature today.

I'm wondering though, in your life, what happens to you when you find obstacles in your way? Do you just sort of cave in, and turn around and quit? Or do you really make the extra effort to climb over or go around them to get to the destination where you want to arrive? It takes work. It takes effort, but it's worth it in the end.

So let me challenge you today to take the extra step. Don't let those little things that stand in the way be obstructions that keep you from accomplishing your life's purpose.

Just a thought for the day. I share it with you today just because I can!

—42—
Road Signs Are Vital

https://www.youtube.com/watch?v=6lB_S6E3pTM

Signs. Stop signs. Street signs. All kinds of signs! Well, they're all important. You drive down the road, and you'll see a speed limit sign. It's there for a purpose. It's there to give us some clarity, some boundaries, some borders to function within. When you come to a stop sign, some with a flashing red light like this one, well of course if you don't stop, you're risking your own life or even someone else's life. So, it's important to listen and obey the stop signs.

In life it's like that. We all have different signs that we need to follow—warning signs or sometimes inner promptings, that small voice within that says, "Ah, this isn't a good thing," or "Don't do that!" Those are the promptings and voices we must listen to inside if we're going to find success in life. Otherwise, we're going to find ourselves sitting in a ditch somewhere off the side of the road, and looking for somebody else to pull us out of the ditch.

Well, I don't want to be there. I want to stay on the main road. I want to keep going straight. I want to make sure my life is on track, and so I'm going to follow the guidelines. That's why I've got a Bible to go by. The Bible gives me some very clear guidelines as to how I should navigate my life. It's got warning signs along the road that will point me in the right direction. It tells me the kinds of friends I should associate with, and the kinds of things I should or should not be doing. Yes, the Bible is my guidebook and my map.

I don't know about you, but I'm glad I've got some kind of a guide to help me around the bends of life and keep me on the road, even when the road may be messy today.

Those are some of my thoughts. I share them with you just because I can!

—43—
Gullywasher!

https://www.youtube.com/watch?v=dCp4UmOf7Ls

Here I am, standing in huge culvert. This culvert is bigger than I am. It's taller than I am. I can't reach the top! If you look behind me, you can see the places where the water has flowed through in the past, and only a little bit is flowing through today.

I'm here because I think this is a good picture of how I'm feeling today. I'm usually a very "up" kind of person, but today is a sad day for me. I feel the weight of it on my shoulders. I feel sadness.

I'm not sure exactly why. Maybe it's all of the COVID-19 restrictions—not being able to go to dinners, have some social time with other people, or be with people outside of your family. Maybe it's a lack of entertainment—going somewhere, getting away somewhere, exploring the community and environment. Maybe that's part of it. I'm not sure!

Maybe the other part of it is the people I'm dealing with as a pastor during the week—people that are sad or at their wits' end. They're not sure where to turn, and come to me looking for hope. Sometimes I wonder at the end of the day if I have actually helped them as I shared with them. Maybe that's part of the weight that I carry. Or maybe it's my own bad decisions that I have made and that I worry about, not having lived up to my own expectations. Or maybe I worry about not living up to the expectations of the people. All of those things might contribute to the fact that I feel this way today.

So coming to this culvert reminds me of hope. In this culvert at the other end, when there's a storm, when it really rains hard, this culvert will be absolutely filled with water, sweeping through here, washing everything away. I'm sort of looking at it saying, "That's what needs to happen for me today." I just need this fresh flow—a fresh flush—that washes everything off my shoulders, refreshes my brain, and washes me clean of all those things that are weighing me down and wearing away at me.

I don't know if you feel that way sometimes or not, but I know this: the word of God doesn't change, and God doesn't change. The scripture says, "Being confident of this very thing—that He who began a good work in you will perform it until the day of Christ."

So I know it's going to be okay tomorrow. I know I'm going to have a better day tomorrow. But until then, I'm going to keep pushing through and trusting in Him.

I have had these thoughts today, and thought that maybe it might be a good thing to share with you, just because I can!

—44—
Amazing Formations

https://www.youtube.com/watch?v=8qjmsIr8kes

I don't suppose that you can see it nearly as clearly as I can, but the beautiful formation of the clouds above my head—the creative work of our God—is so awesome, you can look up one moment and then another moment later it's a completely new design! God is at work, working at a master's speed, just creating and recreating new designs every moment. A little breeze that we feel here is a huge wind in the sky, realigning the clouds and painting a new picture.

I think that's what God does with each of us. He's working in us, he's transforming us, he's allowing the winds to blow to change us. To reform us. These winds are sent to create in us something beautiful. Now, from our perspective, we can't see exactly what he sees, but he is working in us to do something amazing.

The next time you look up to the clouds, watch the sky, and watch the formation of the clouds. Every once in a while, you'll see the life go by, like one of the birds that just flew by a little earlier. It's great! God's work is amazing! There's so much life out there that we don't even see.

Well, when you think of it, think of the amazing God we serve—the creator of the universe, and He's my Father!

I share this with you today just because I can.

—45— New Beauty Daily

https://www.youtube.com/watch?v=PcZVjLkAK_A

I never cease to be amazed at the beauty of God's creation! Here I am at Little Lake Park in Midland, Ontario. I'm just taking a bit of a holiday—a holy day—one day apart to visit and view the beautiful creation that God has given to us.

I'm always overwhelmed at the beauty of nature. It's hard to understand how the God who is able to create these kinds of scenes—every day a new day, a new scene—is interested in us personally. How awesome to know that this kind of a God is the God who looks down on us and sees us as we are. He loves us, and embraces us, and wants to have a personal relationship with us. It's amazing. It's awe-inspiring. It's unbelievable. He wants to have a relationship with us, and he counts us as his highest form of creation.

I'm just in awe today of his great love and his creative ability. I'm sharing it with you today just because I can!

—46— My Treehouse

https://www.youtube.com/watch?v=WeID-_4WnsQ

Wow! Treehouses. This one is a two-storey treehouse. Awesome! When my kids were younger, we built a treehouse, and I thought it was just awesome. It was enclosed, it had a bit of a lookout, and a staircase going up to it in our backyard in the city of Barrie, Ontario, and it was an awesome treehouse!

As fathers, what we do for kids is amazing. We do anything to make sure our kids are happy and enjoy life, and if it's a treehouse in the backyard, of course we want to do that!

A parallel—what about God the Father for us? The homes we live in now are like a treehouse from him. Oh, they're beautiful, they're homes, they're full-time, year-round homes that we live in, but in comparison to what he's got for us, it's only a treehouse. Ever thought about that? It's amazing!

Jesus said, "In my Father's house are many mansions. I go to prepare a place for you, and if I go to prepare a place for you, I will come again and receive you unto myself."

I hope that you are prepared for your eternal mansion. It's going to be a lot better than just a treehouse. It's a lot nicer than the mansion you might be living in now, down here on earth. It will be a great place. The Father, as loving fathers want to make good places for our kids, is building a better place for us, and our present home is nothing in comparison to our future home. Today's home is just a treehouse.

Just a few thoughts I thought I'd share with you today, just because I can!

—47—

Make This Moment Count!

https://www.youtube.com/watch?v=sBDDn6gBuxQ

It's a windy day here in the cemetery, I found myself here at a cemetery in Innisfil, Ontario. There are a lot of people in this cemetery that I have actually conducted their funerals and buried them. I thought I'd stop and share a few thoughts about this cemetery.

Everybody behind me has expired. The fact that you're reading this today and you're able to see this is evidence that you haven't expired yet! You have got this moment to live in your life.

I want to challenge you today: enjoy this moment, and make the best of this moment, because you don't know how long you've got—maybe tomorrow, maybe a month, maybe a few years. Whatever it is, it's going to be too short, we know that for sure! So enjoy this moment.

Make your life count. Don't waste time fooling around or messing around doing the wrong stuff and getting into trouble. No, make this moment count because it's given to you as a gift from the creator, God above.

And make sure you're ready! Ready for the day you have someone else drive you into a place like this to bury you forever.

I'm sharing these few thoughts with you today to "make this moment count!" And I'm sharing it with you just because I can!

—48—
Time for a Good Deed

https://www.youtube.com/watch?v=uRplc3760Fs

Today was a special day for us in Innisfil, because one of our local council members, Councillor Orsatti, who lives just around the corner from where we live, put on a garage sale!

And it wasn't just any old garage sale. This garage sale was 100 percent for charity—50 percent going to the Innisfil Food Bank and the remaining 50 percent going to the Gilda's Club.

We're so thankful for a councillor that really cares about the community and wants to invest in the most vulnerable people by serving these charities.

It's something for us to think about. What are you doing to help the community become a more positive place and better service the needs in your town? You can do something! The old saying was, “a good deed a day.” Well, it doesn’t have to be one like this one every day, but it’s worth thinking about. How about doing a good deed every day–helping somebody out, sharing with someone in need, or simply highlighting a charity that’s doing a good work in the community?

I’m so thankful for Councillor Orsatti’s work today and those who helped her make this a success, and we look forward to serving the most vulnerable in our community through the Innisfil Food Bank.

Support those around you. Do a good deed today. I’m sharing this with you today just because I can.

—49— Time to Give Thanks

https://www.youtube.com/watch?v=pE-ZyhRjEDE

Happy thanksgiving! It's harvest time. It's a great time of the year to give thanks to God for all that he's given to us—our food, our shelter, our clothing, our friends, our family. There are just so many things that God has given to us! And what a great country to live in at this particular time.

At harvest time here in Innisfil, Ontario, these corn stalks have grown. They've produced the cobs of corn on them, and it's drying out, getting ready for harvest. This farmer knows exactly what time to begin to put in the harvester and reap it.

Like the farmer, we've all got some significance that we need to offer to others in the community. Thanksgiving! Be thankful for what you have, but don't store it up inside—don't keep it inside. Develop that ability to help others, to share your abilities with others. Encourage people to become a significant impact in your own community. You can do it! God's placed you here for that. You've got purpose! You don't need to lose hope, because there are so many more people that need you at this particular time, in this season.

Happy thanksgiving! Be a significant influence in others' lives, and have a great holiday weekend!

I share this with you today just because I can.

—50— What's a FOSC?

https://www.youtube.com/watch?v=GDUNEycV68E

You probably haven't paid much attention to these before, but you might see them as you drive down the highway. Between the hydro poles you'll see these cylinders strung from the wires between the hydro poles. Every once in a while, you might see one of these just sitting there, or sometimes you'll see a loop of wire that goes into them. There are usually two loops—one going in, and one going out.

It is a FOSC—a "fiber optic splice closure." This is where the connections are made from one wire to the next, if you're connecting two wires. It's part of the infrastructure of our community. It is so important that if this isn't there, you've got no internet, you've got no connection, you've got no phone. You're just dead in the water, so to speak. These are significant components of the infrastructure of our municipality, and in fact, of the world.

As I thought about these fiber optic splice closures, I thought how important it is for us to recognize that we've got a connection—not in one of these plastic containers—we have a connection to heaven through prayer. We don't need one of these connections. We already have a connection—a vertical connection with God. So often we don't use it.

You know what happens when your internet's down, or when it's slow, or when your phone's out? You miss it tremendously. Why isn't it like that in our vertical relationship? God is waiting to commune with us. He wants us to talk with him. He wants to hear from us. He wants to have an impact in our lives as we share together back and forth in communication with him. He speaks to us we speak to him. Infrastructure—vertically, heavenward—and you can make use of it!

The next time you see one of these, remember it's a "FOSC." That's what it is called, and now you know what it does.

I share this with you today just because I can!

—51—
Are You Technically Overwhelmed?

https://www.youtube.com/watch?v=xLw3CUM3QFI

Good morning! Here I am at Innisfil Community Church, where I am the pastor. I'm inside the sanctuary of the church, and directly behind me is our sound and tech room. It's located right at the back of the sanctuary.

Let me just give you a little insight. On one side we have our soundboard. It's fully digital and it's got a lot of options on it. It's sometimes hard to get volunteers to operate this because it seems to be complex and difficult to understand sometimes because it's modern and digital.

Of course, we're in a digital age and everybody's online somewhere, so in the center area of this room there's another console. This is our streaming console. We have three video monitors here, and a volunteer sits here and monitors it, switches the cameras, and makes sure the sound going out to the live stream is right. This is so that people who are not able to get to church can watch the service from home.

On the other side of this room, we have another set of three monitors along with a separate computer system. This is what projects the lyrics onto the screen at the front of the sanctuary so that we can sing along with the words in-house. Churches used to have hymn books, but we don't have hymn books anymore, and everything's live. It's on the live stream and it's digitally projected on the screen so you watch the words and sing along that way.

So much has changed. I've been in the ministry for over 40 years, maybe almost 50 years or something like that, and everything's changed since I entered the ministry. Sometimes it can be overwhelming. Sometimes it just boggles the mind how much change is happening! All of this technology!

But I want you to know the one thing that hasn't changed, and that's God himself! The God who wants to have a relationship with you. The God who cares for you. The God who loves you intimately. He has not changed the Bible, which says Jesus Christ is the same yesterday, today, and forever. He cares for you. He loves you! That's the one secure thing in your life!

So when you get frightened with all the technology and you can't figure it out, remember your relationship with God hasn't changed. You can still talk to him the same way you did 50 years ago, 60 years ago, or 70 years ago. Some of the older saints I've talked to are so grateful that they have relationship with God, and that they know that God still hears them, and that God still answers prayer.

I believe it's still true! He hears us. He answers our prayers! And I just thought—in the midst of all of the changes that are happening these days, in this new era that we're living in—I'd share this with you today, just because I can!

—52— In Amazement, or Just a Maze?

https://www.youtube.com/watch?v=VRcjS5CEsGk

Here I am, pointing out to you some of the connections to the internet from our church. All of the wires! Wires going everywhere! Through the walls and the building, cables all over the place. Many of them are cables for security cameras, security alarms, or wired internet connections for all of our computers.

In behind all of the wires, if you look closely, there is a little black connection. It's difficult to see, but from this little black connection comes a little thread of a wire. In fact, it's not truly a wire, but glass fiber that comes from that connection. This is what connects us to the world wide web. Everything we do on the computers, everything that we transmit in and out of the building, all of our live streaming, goes through that little thin fiber connection that we have to the internet.

The speed is absolutely amazing. It's fast. When I was watching it being installed today, I just sort of stood back in amazement. I wonder if in our society we have lost that sense of wonder, that sense of amazement. Some of these things are just amazing, and that's the lightest way we can say it. It's so complex, and yet so simple—so small.

I wonder how many things in life we pass by without standing back and finding that moment of amazement. How often do we take a moment to admire God's creative hand in making the little things so significant and so important? He also gives to us a little bit of insight—a little bit of knowledge—about how to tap into some of these things, and to make them work for us in a variety of ways.

I don't know about you, but I just stood back in amazement to think that through this little glass thread all of our technology is connected to the world wide web, and we can go around the world with our live stream, and all of the other stuff we do because of this connection. it's amazing!

I'm sharing this with you today just because I can!

—53—
Markers & Monuments

https://www.youtube.com/watch?v=8Ky8Vu3iT1Q

I'm here in Belle Ewart, a hamlet in the town of Innisfil. I'm standing outside of the Royal Canadian Legion, a branch here in Belle Ewart. On one part of their property a number of years ago, they established this particular monument—this particular marker—to remember those who have given of themselves or who are serving currently in the military. In this particular branch, No. 547, of the Legion, there's a statement that's always read at Remembrance Day services, throughout generations: "At the going down of the sun, and in the morning, we will remember them."

We build these markers and monuments to remember significant moments and significant lives—moments and lives of particular significance that need a remembrance so we don't forget them.

I think in our spiritual journey it's also important for us to make monuments and establish markers in our journey of faith. In our particular tradition as Christians, we would say one of those solid markers is the moment you decide to serve Jesus Christ and to live your life as a Christian. At that moment you become a follower of Jesus Christ and base your life and morals on the basis of scripture, the Holy Bible. That's a marker so secure in our lives that we can go back to that moment at any point in time and say, "Yes, I surrendered my life to Christ." It's like building a monument just like this one, saying, "That moment was significant."

I think we all need to establish markers in life. We can look back and have the security of knowing where we've been, where we're going, what we've decided, and how we're going to get there.

Monuments—markers—in your life. What are the spiritual markers in your journey? Can you point back to that particular time and that particular place where a significant thing happened in your spiritual journey? When and where did you decide to follow Christ? I think it's so important to have that security of looking back and saying, "Yes, at that time, I chose to do this."

Markers are important, and we're remembering some of those in these days.

I share this with you today just because I can!

—54—
No Man Is an Island

https://www.youtube.com/watch?v=zH1dLgfrn-k

Here I am again at Innisfil Beach Park in the town of Innisfil, Ontario. It's a great spot. It's a gem in our community, a park that's so beautiful. Just out beyond my shoulder is an island, and this island is accessible only by boat.

It's interesting, I was thinking of the saying, "No man is an island unto himself," and I thought, you know, it's so true—no matter how alone we are, we're really never alone. There are many ways that people have access into our lives, and ways that we have access into other people's lives to connect with them.

This is a time where we really need to connect with one another. Whether you connect by phone, text, or whether you jump in a boat and go to somebody else's place from an island, or whether you drop by someone's house to chat on the front porch, we need to connect.

No man is an island unto himself. We need each other. You need somebody in your life, and somebody else needs you in their life. So take time today to think of some ways that you can be a bridge to somebody who's feeling like they're an island off by themselves and that nobody cares. You can do something good today!

I'm sharing this with you today just because I can.

—55—
Darkness Hides the Good . . . Temporarily

https://www.youtube.com/watch?v=hTmhy4tJI0c

The sound of water splashing on the shoreline;
Looking across the beauty of the water,
Not far from where we live.

It's gorgeous, and such a beautiful day, but all of this beauty can be covered up with the darkness at night. All of a sudden, we lose sight of the beauty and the gorgeous creation that God has made.

Sometimes life is like that. When we're in the midst of darkness, it's hard to see the beauty all around us. The beauty gets lost. In this time of darkness and despair that our country is facing—that our world is facing—it's easy to get lost in the darkness.

But let me suggest that there is still the beauty beneath the darkness! We see here the vastness of the water, the beauty of the sky, the sun shining so bright. It's wonderful! We hear the sounds of the water splashing on the shore. They're all still there, if we can just look past the circumstances around us.

Don't let the darkness destroy the hope. Don't let the darkness destroy your life and your feeling of well-being. Dig beneath the darkness. Look beyond, and you'll see the beauty all around you.

I'm sharing these thoughts with you today just because I can!

—56—
Time to Laugh

https://www.youtube.com/watch?v=L6-wyWEkLX8

Our neighbours to the south of us in the USA have just been through a very challenging and difficult election. Although they are south of us, it did engage a lot of our people in discussions and debates. There's no end to all that's transpired—conspiracy theories and all—but it's nice to be able to look back and say, "That chapter is over," and to smile and have a laugh now and again. That's one of the things we've missed—a little bit of laughter in the midst of all of the challenges that have been happening, all of the stresses of life, and with the pandemic often robbing us of joy.

Sometimes we just need a good laugh! Laughing at yourself. Finding a moment of joy. Finding a moment of expression. It's amazing what laughter does for us! It's a stress reliever. It helps us through the day. How many times do you laugh at yourself during the day? How many times do you laugh at circumstances? It's a sign of good health. It releases tension. It gives better mental health. And it just helps us through the day! So stop sometime during the day, and make sure you have a good laugh. It's worth it!

I'm sharing this with you today just because I can!

—57—
Up Against A Wall

https://www.youtube.com/watch?v=_7Cyy6A_Tso

Here I am with the children of Israel, back in history. Yes, they were being chased by their enemies. They were on their journey to the promised land, but they came to a place at the Red Sea where there's no road left for them. They're at the end of the road. The end of the rope. There's nowhere to go. Their enemies are pursuing them and pressing in behind them. They're about to be overtaken. They're lost! There is nowhere to go until, of course, God speaks.

Moses strikes the Red Sea and the Red Sea parts. There are walls of water on either side—the water spontaneously stands up—something that probably never happened in history before! And there's a path made through the Red Sea where the Israelites cross the Red Sea on dry ground! They don't get stuck in mud and the mire—no, this is *dry* ground that God has prepared for them. They cross through successfully, and arrive on the other side safe from their enemies.

I don't know about you, but in the day we're living in, this season of difficulty, you may feel like you're up against a wall with nowhere to go and nowhere to turn. You don't know how you're going to get through this. You think you're ready to die because there's nowhere to go. But wait, you can do the same thing they did! Now don't just whisper a prayer. No, *shout out* to God, "God, I need you! I need your help!"

It's amazing how God might respond to you. Maybe like he did for the Israelites, he'll part the Red Sea for you and make a way where there was no way. He overrides the natural circumstances and imparts the supernatural, and suddenly there's a way. I've been there before, when God parted the paths for me. He made a way where there was no way.

I don't know about you. Maybe you're facing a wall of depression, or a wall of financial insecurity, or a wall of isolation, or maybe you're just feeling alone. Whatever it is that you're up against, you can call out to God and see what he might do for you. It's amazing! This is a great story.

I wanted to share it with you today just because I can.

—58—
Use the Dumpster

https://www.youtube.com/watch?v=Q0Gbs0jTOs8

What kinds of words and descriptions come to you when you see this pile of garbage? What does it evoke in your mind? Certainly, there's a lot of waste. In this dumpster there may be a lot of textiles, old clothes, expired or extra food, or maybe even some old furniture that's left over from a house or a warehouse.

We're not going to do any dumpster diving tonight to check out what's in there, but what I'm thinking is that in a spiritual way, all of us will find certain things in our lives that are garbage. Things that need to be tossed into a dumpster. Maybe there are some old hurts that you've been hanging on to that have been holding you back and causing you pain. Maybe there's someone that said some nasty stuff to you. Maybe these things have sort of debilitated you, and now you think you can't do anything, or at least you can't do anything right.

Some of those things you need to dig inside of you and find out what they are. It's garbage inside of you that you need to take and dump over your shoulder into a dumpster! You might even want to visually take that thing—whatever you have that comes to your mind that's holding you back—that's garbage in your life and literally walk over to a dumpster and toss it in, because sometimes the imagery helps us let go of junk.

It's not easy to let go of junk. There are lots of people, and many of us are not good at decluttering many times, and certainly not in our spiritual life. So I'm challenging you today, as you think about this, dig down inside of you. Find out what those things are that are holding you back and are hindering you from moving forward. If you don't toss them into the dumpster soon, you're going to have a lot of wasted time, perhaps some wasted years.

Yeah, dig down real deep, find it, toss it, and move on.

I'm sharing this with you today just because I can.

—59— A Dilapidated House

https://www.youtube.com/watch?v=t27JjaczTQM

This vacant house in the community is really an interesting spot. I'm going to take a walk through it now, and you can follow me along. We're going to make an entry into the main entranceway. You can see it's pretty well mangled up and broken up. There's a lot of junk along the way. We're going to take a walk on the inside. Let's take a look and see what we've got.

There's a staircase in this vacant house. We walk into a bedroom, and it's a rather interesting spot, with clothes still left on the floor. There are some windows that are broken out. There's nothing really happening there, but take a look here—we've got a bed already ready made. Ready to sleep in! It looks like somebody's been using this on a regular basis here. At the end of the hallway is a staircase. On the ceiling here is an active smoke detector. It's working! We're in the next room again, and when I walk through in these spots, it's really a bit of a mess. The kitchen is pretty well gone.

What kind of a spiritual application can we make with this house in mind? I look at this house and think how often people look on the outside and it looks really interesting, but inside it's really dingy and in really bad shape.

What about your life? What about the interior portions of your life? In the interior cavities of your life, what's hidden inside? What is messy and really isn't good for you that you need to clean up?

I know it's not easy to take a look sometimes. It's hard to look. You can't stand the inside, just like in this dilapidated building, but there's the intrigue of the outside that looks great. Are you wondering what's inside? Only you know what might be inside your heart or inside your life that you're covering up that on the outside. What are you covering up? Maybe today would be a good day to look inside and say, "Okay God, maybe there's some stuff I need to change. Maybe I need to deal with some of that stuff, and get rid of the garbage, and clean up my 'house.'"

It's just a thought, in a moment of intrigue, my thought for the day.

I'm sharing it with you today just because I can!

—60—
The Old Grain Elevator

https://www.youtube.com/watch?v=ZDjhujd-I6s

Right behind me is a piece of history of our town, in the town of Innisfil, Ontario. This grain elevator has been here for a long time, but now as you might be able to see, it's in the process of demolition. Some things just don't stay the same. No doubt this grain elevator has been replaced by something much better and more efficient, handling in different ways the same products at a different location.

It's often hard for us to accept change. It's hard for us to see something that's been established and in town for so long demolished, but change is part of life.

I wonder what kind of things you're holding on to in your life. Are there structures and systems that you're stuck on that are holding you back from being more effective, more efficient, and being better, and doing better? Some of those systems, some of those structures, of how you think, or how you do things—maybe they need to change. Maybe some of the systems that are established in your life are holding you back from really being the best you that you can be! So take a look, do some introspection today, and see what structures or systems need to change in your life.

I know that with Black History Month (the month of February in Canada) coming to a conclusion, our thinking processes haven't always been that clear, and we need to make some changes in how we think and live. Maybe that's true in other areas of your life too.

I'm sharing this with you today just because I can.

Life will go on!

—61—
The Great White Throne

https://www.youtube.com/watch?v=7Gsarnssu9c

Welcome to the great white throne . . . in our house. We all need toilets. I observed over the last while that I could hear the water running very softly throughout the night and in the daytime, and I wondered where this toilet was leaking.

At first, I thought maybe the seal was gone, where the water was escaping into the toilet bowl. Instead what I found when I took it apart was that one particular part—the refill kit—was not shutting off totally. There it was, defective, and letting a slow but constant flow of water down the drain. Of course, that extra water is added onto my bill every month. So I need to replace this. In true handyman style, I've got a new one to put in and it should stop this ongoing leak.

As I considered that, I wondered what things are in our life that are like that—they are just a constant drain on you. It's something that just constantly runs in the background. You don't realize you're doing it. You don't realize it's happening. At the end of the day, you've wasted a lot of energy, and a lot of time, and probably a lot of potential. It's probably robbed you of your joy and sapped you of your energy. By ignoring it, you're really flushing all your energy, all of that good stuff, down the toilet. It even costs you to get rid of it! The municipality charges us for the water that comes into the house and the water that goes out of the house—double! They get us coming and going, both ways.

Well maybe it's worthwhile to again take an introspective look. Are there some things in your life that are constant drains for you? Things that you just need to replace? Perhaps you need to put a new part in, or you need to do something different. Perhaps you need to adjust your ways of doing things so that you can use that energy—use that life—to do something productive and meaningful, and find your joy all over again, in a new dimension.

Well, that's a handyman special for today. I'm sharing it with you just because I can.

—62—
The Seventh Line Tunnel

https://www.youtube.com/watch?v=FuyY5Hmf3Eg

I'm on the Seventh Line at Highway 11 in Innisfil, Ontario. It's got to be my favorite spot in Innisfil for its scenery. This particular road is a rather interesting road. It's grown over, and in some places, it seems like it's almost a tunnel, where the trees merge together overtop of us. I can just picture coming down with a horse and buggy through this tunnel on the Seventh Line.

It's beautiful now, but things are changing in the immediate future here. The municipality has decided that this road needs to be widened, and these trees on either side have to be removed in order to accommodate a road that is accessible. So, in these next few days and weeks, this is going to be under construction.

Now, I know it's hard when things change like this, but this road is a narrow road and it's limiting in terms of how many people can use it. Right now, for safety reasons, only the residents can use it. Our municipality wants to expand it so that it can become a usable road and others can have access to it. The boundaries need to be expanded and the borders have to be pushed back.

I wonder if that's what happens in our own lives sometimes. We get traveling down a narrow path, a narrow viewpoint, that eliminates other people from coming alongside of us, because our thinking has become too narrow or too limited. It's not broad enough to include them.

I wonder if we need to do the same thing in our own lives—push back the boundaries, expand our thinking to embrace others who do not think the same way as we do, who may not look or sound the same as we do, or who may not govern the same way as we might. Pushing back those boundaries does not mean betraying your own value system. You don't have to give up your values for it. You give up your understanding to a broader understanding, to a more widened perspective, so you can understand them better, and you can understand the world better.

I think we need to do that in many areas. I don't want to travel a narrow road that's limited and miss opportunities to speak into the lives of others who are unlike me. I need people that are unlike me so I can grow, and push my limits, and push my boundaries beyond where I'm at. I recognize there are times I'm going to have to push back a little bit, stand my ground, and maintain my value system, but I don't have to betray who I am to embrace their thinking and begin to understand how they think.

I'm sharing it with you today, an illustration from this road—the Seventh Line that's soon going to be expanded—sharing it with you today just because I can!

—63—
A Taste of Easter

https://www.youtube.com/watch?v=AlXbEj63PNU

It was a number of years ago when we came up with a thought and idea that this municipality needs some images of the Christian faith in the community, because according to Statistics Canada, our community is predominantly Christian. So, we erected these three crosses with the approval of the Innisfil Arts & Culture and Heritage Committee. They approved this as a piece of art for our municipality.

Most people don't know that. Also, most people don't realize that we don't celebrate the Christian faith as much as some other organizations or some other faiths do. We don't do well in celebrating our faith. Christmas and Easter are probably the two celebrations that we do the best, but we still don't do a good job. Many people don't realize that Easter for us is really the crux of our spiritual lives, because it was on this middle cross where we believe Jesus Christ paid the price for our sins.

Jesus died on the cross to make available to us forgiveness and cleansing from all of our sins, past, present, and future. If we call on him, and invite him to forgive us, we believe he will totally remove that load of guilt upon our shoulders—a load we can't do anything with except carry it. But Jesus came along and said, "I want to forgive you. I want to help you on the road, and I can give you forgiveness if you come to me." On the cross, he paid the penalty for all of our sins. That's worth celebrating! It's a season to celebrate!

On either of the other two crosses, there were two convicted criminals. One cried out to Jesus, and Jesus responded to him with forgiveness and said, "Today you'll be in paradise with me." The other one rejected Jesus and ended up suffering the penalty of sin, ultimately dying in his sins, forever separated from God, as we understand from scripture.

The Easter season. It's a wonderful season to celebrate, and I hope that you can just take a few moments and celebrate it with those in the Christian faith around you. We can be so grateful, so thankful, for a saviour, Jesus Christ, who loved us and gave himself for us. That's what we believe! It is written in the holy scriptures, and we believe it wholeheartedly.

I share this with you today just because I can!

—64—
It Takes a Team

https://www.youtube.com/watch?v=O_BxOFSExNc

None of us really wants to end up in the emergency department at the hospital, but unexpected emergencies happen all the time. In our lives we are subject to all kinds of things that are unforeseen. When it happens, we want to make sure there are people in place to help us. Whether it is the paramedics who are transporting us, or the first responders who were there before the paramedics arrived, or the staff at the hospital, they all play an important role in our health care system. They are so important. There are so many people behind the scenes.

In a church, it's the same way. Church is not just a building. Church is a group of people, working together in a variety of places doing a variety of activities making sure we properly care for the spiritual needs of individuals. In our community, that means reaching out to people with mental health issues, physical needs, and social needs; connecting with people, visiting people who are isolated; visiting people who are sick; speaking to those in prison, and somehow connecting with them and helping to re-establish themselves in the community. All of these things are ministries that the church works together on—individuals working together for the common good in our community in the world around us.

What kind of a role do you play in that network of people? It's important. We all have a role to play, and you need to do your part to make this world a better place.

If you are not already involved, step up to the plate, volunteer. get involved somewhere, and help us improve our world.

I'm sharing this with you today just because I can.

—65—
Stumped—'Only One Way?'

https://www.youtube.com/watch?v=MotHYkwpaic

Okay, I'm stumped! How tall or how short does a trunk of a tree have to be in order to be called a "stump"? I'm not sure about the answer to that, but there are all kinds of questions like these.

In the journey of the Christian faith, there are other things we can get stumped about. One of those is, "Is there really only one way to get to heaven? Only one way to God?"

"Well, of course," some people say. "There are a multitude of ways!"

That's sort of like saying that your vehicle runs on liquid fuel, so why not fill it up with water, or apple juice, or milk? After all, every liquid leads to fuel. Not so! I can't even put diesel fuel in my truck. I need gasoline.

So why is it so difficult for us to understand that there has to be one way that it works? Only gasoline!

And so it is with the Christian faith. There are not many ways to heaven. There is only one way that works! Jesus said, "I am the way, the truth, and the life, no man comes to the Father but by me."

If you're stumped by these types of questions, read the Book and you won't be stumped any longer.

I'm sharing it with you today just because I can.

—66—
Stumped—'The Trinity'

https://www.youtube.com/watch?v=DbWMe2ntrrM

Stumped! This tree is stumped. Well, what's left of it is a stump. It's maybe a little taller than some stumps, but it's a stump. I'm sure this tree could tell lots of stories. If this tree could tell you the stories, it would tell you of many branches, and many limbs. In fact, I can see the remains of some of them!

How often are you stumped in your Christian faith? What kind of questions do you have, but are not able to answer them completely? What kind of things do you not understand totally, but you want to understand in light of the truth of scripture?

Well, the Trinity is one of those things that stumps a lot of people. People don't understand the Trinity, so I think the best illustration that

I've come across is the illustration of water. Water—H_2O—exists in a multitude of forms: ice, running water (like a stream), or vapour (like steam or clouds). There are many forms. I like ice, water, and steam to explaining the Trinity because all three are identical. They're H_2O. None diminishes the value of the other. None is distinguished differently than the other except in its manifestation, or the way it presents itself.

I think that's a good picture of God the Holy Spirit, God the Father, and God the Son—three in one, yet there's only one God. One true God. I thought, if you're stumped about some of these things, there are some answers. Oh, we don't know it all—we'll get stumped from time to time—but there are some simple explanations that can help us at least understand in part.

I'm sharing this with you today just because I can.

—67—
Stumped—'A Second Coming?'

https://www.youtube.com/watch?v=1mdm4sQX4wg

Recently stumped. That's right, this tree—three significantly sized trunks—stumped. Have you ever felt stumped? Well, there are lots of things that stump people's minds.

I was thinking of the second coming of Jesus Christ. There are lots of stories, lots of accounts, lots of variations, in how the story is told, but sometimes it just stumps us to think, "How could this be? How could Jesus Christ come back again?"

In the scriptures, there are more prophecies of the second coming of Jesus than the first coming! And yet, the first coming of Jesus happened exactly as predicted in scriptures. It stumped a lot of people then! They wondered, "How could it be?" Even the disciples didn't really understand it completely. They were stumped. Especially when Jesus was crucified!

So, yeah, it's not strange that we're stumped from time to time, especially when we think of these challenging scriptural accounts that Jesus is coming back again. How could that be? Well, even if you're stumped, the prophecies are still true. It will happen as the scriptures say, and there's more evidence of the second coming of Jesus than the first, so I believe it's going to happen, and it may happen sooner than we believe it could! So, don't be stumped any longer. Hey, look in the Book, read it for yourself. Discover the truth, and you won't be stumped any longer.

I'm sharing it with you today just because I can!

—68—
Stumped—'The Resurrection'

https://www.youtube.com/watch?v=Gsloh4WZVMo

Stumped! Underneath this these young branches is a stump that has been here for years, but the amazing thing is that new growth is beginning to come out of it! There are buds on the tree now. There is brand new growth!

I know you've been stumped about a lot of things in life. Some people are stumped about theological things. This stump reminds me of the resurrection. When this tree was cut down and stumped, no one expected it to grow again. It was done. It was finished. But then, years later, all of a sudden, new life began to bloom and grow from the stump!

To me, that's a picture of the resurrection. Jesus died, was placed in the grave, and everybody thought it was over. Then later—three days later—he breaks forth from the grave. This was a rather rapid resurrection!

You and I have also been promised a resurrection. Those who trust in Jesus will be resurrected unto eternal life. Those who are not followers of Jesus will be resurrected onto a place of judgment and condemnation. So when you struggle with truths like the resurrection, and wonder how it can happen, just take a look at some of the old stumps and see the new growth that comes much later. It's amazing!

I thought I'd share this with you today just because I can!

—69—
Stumped—Inside Discovery

https://www.youtube.com/watch?v=B-IlaJhTl9E

Wow! Another stump! Can you believe it? Inside this stump is a total image of a human vertebrae—a human spine! It's amazing! From the very bottom to the top. Who would have ever known this was inside of this stump! But somebody, somehow, said, "I'm going to see what's inside," and they began to open up this stump and discover it inside. This human spine—inside a stump–it's amazing!

Top to bottom, bottom to top, it's unbelievable!

Okay, well, you and I know that it wasn't really a human vertebrae spine in there. Somehow a master craftsman came along and said, "I can see something in that stump that nobody else can see, and I'm going to carve it out."

That's exactly what God does for us. He sees in us the potential of his beauty, and he begins to chip away and make something beautiful of our lives. It may not be a human spine or vertebrae like this, but it's something beautiful. He's chipping away at you, and if you just let him, it's amazing what he'll do in your life!

I thought I'd share this with you today just because I can.

—70—
Be Part of Something Good!

https://www.youtube.com/watch?v=vAzW3qUnFFM

Here in the town of Innisfil, Ontario, we are so blessed to have some wonderful organizations and wonderful people who really care for their community. They really support the residents that live around us. The Rotary Club is one of those clubs. This club includes many individuals who do this, and the beautiful thing about the Rotary Club is that there's a four-way test that they use in their organization as they endeavour to support others.

The basic question, "Is it the truth?" This is a solid foundation.

A second, "Is it fair to all concerned?"

They also ask the question, "Would it be good for the betterment of friendships?"

Finally, "Would be beneficial to all?"

These are some very basic things that the Rotary Club stands for. It's just common sense to say, "let's make this community a better community."

This flower bed is one of their projects. This particular flower bed is at the entrance to the local community recreation center. They've planted all these flowers. I saw them out here working away some time ago doing it, and here we are at a beautiful flower garden that's going to look even better in the days to come! They put lots of work and effort into it.

I'm wondering about you. Are you committed to your local community? Are you involved in doing something significant to help make it a better place? We've got such a great community, but we need people that are going to help us keep it strong and keep it together. To be a kind, caring community takes all of us to do it.

I'm challenging you today if you're not already involved in some kind of a group, maybe a church group, or a local club organization that's doing good for the community, it's the right thing to do! For me, it's part of my faith. My faith says to love one another. "Love your neighbor as yourself."

And so, I'm involved in a variety of things, and I'm certainly strongly supportive of this organization, the local Innisfil Rotary Club. They've been a great partner to us as a church and as a food bank, and it's such a valuable asset to be part of one another, doing great things in the community. So lock in, find a place that you fit with, get in, support it, build your community, and it will build your life and make it better as you go.

I'm sharing these thoughts with you today just because I can!

—71—
A Deadly Bore!

https://www.youtube.com/watch?v=AQkFZSHKMw4

Here's one of those trees in our town that has suffered from disease over the last several months. Our municipality has come by and marked an "x" on this particular tree on the boulevard outside of our property. This "x" means that this tree is going to be torn down, sawn, and removed, because it's dead or at least dying.

It has been affected, from what I understand, by the ash borer. What happens is the insects have bored into this tree, drilling into it in multiple places. It is really a bit of a mess when you see the actual holes that are bored right inside of this tree, and has ultimately caused the death of this tree.

I was thinking about that. Sometimes in our lives, we will allow certain things to enter into our lives that do the same thing spiritually as this ash borer does to this tree, causing death. We allow sinful things to come into our lives, that eat away at us inside like a cancer, and ultimately destroy the spiritual life that God has given to us. I think it's so important that we take time to examine our lives, to take a look and internalize some of that stuff, and say, "Is there an opportunity for some kind of thing to enter my spiritual life that might destroy me from within?" Maybe it's an attitude. Maybe it's an action. Maybe it's a behaviour. I mean, maybe it's just all the false teaching that we're swallowing up so quickly and not really paying attention to! Maybe it's a culture we're living in that's overcoming our spiritual lives.

Whatever it is, we need to be so careful we don't let deadly things enter into our life, because we don't want to get cut down and thrown away and thrown into the fire at the end, like this tree will.

Just another wild thought to share with you, just because I can. Have a great day!

—72—
Life's Ups & Downs

https://www.youtube.com/watch?v=8XfTGOU58us

Hey, we all experience life in a variety of ways. There's ups and downs in life for all of us. Here at Innisfil Beach Park there's a new "pump track." Ups and downs here are a lot of fun! There's lots of variety—hit these ramps at whatever speed you want and sometimes you can make air with them. A great time!

It's sort of a new thing here at the park, but in our own lives isn't that the way it is? We all have our ups and downs. Sometimes we don't plan them that way, and sometimes they really take us for a ride—sometimes not in a good way. But, hey, we learn to overcome! We experience the valleys, we experience the hills, but in the end, we make it through. When I look back on life—all of its ups and downs—hey, it's been pretty good, and I'm so thankful for all the ups and downs in my life. It's made me into who I am. I've come through them!

And yeah, sometimes they're a lot of fun. So take some time out of your life to enjoy the ups and downs. It's a great experience! Get some exercise, and get doing something—you might be surprised how good you feel about it!

I'm sharing it with you today just because I can!

—73—
Many Paths, One Destiny

https://www.youtube.com/watch?v=KsCACsXVq5E

Hey! I'm out cruising today on my motorcycle, taking a few moments out on a different mode of transportation. I don't get out on my bike very often, but I like to get out a few times in the summer. As I'm riding around today, I'm thinking about all of the different modes of transportation that people have—skateboards, bicycles, motorcycles, cars, pickup trucks, buses, trains. There are all kinds of modes of transportation, and they all get you to the same end—the destination where you're going! They all work differently, but they're all means to get you to a destination.

I was thinking about that, and I was thinking about all of the different churches we have. There are so many different churches, but again the goal is to get you to your destination—to make sure you end up in heaven, and to make sure you have a spiritual journey that has a path that's meaningful and exciting for you. There are so many churches in our community that would love to have you as part of them. If you're not already engaged in one of the local churches, we would welcome you to any of them in our community. This is a great time for you to reconnect, and a time when we really need connection together. We need to develop mentally, spiritually, and socially. Yes, the social connection has been missing for so long with this pandemic, but it's now time for us to begin to get back together in a safe manner, and if you're not already locked into a church, we would welcome you to join with us!

It's an interesting perspective. We have different modes of transportation, and different modes of churches, all to get us to the same destination—a relationship to God, a relationship with people, and actually, eternity in heaven is the final destination.

I'm sharing this with you today just because I can!

—74—
Alive—Just Because

https://www.youtube.com/watch?v=4RdsBPvYml8

Well, this is just one of those times where I need to reflect on the week that's gone by. Monday morning, I decided that there were some trees on the church property that needed to be trimmed up, and I began to do the work. I trimmed up four trees with a chainsaw, and cut the lower limbs off. I needed to do this to make room for the snow plowing in the wintertime, so the snow can be plowed underneath them and past them.

I finished doing the sawing, put the saw on the back of my pickup truck, and then moved around to the other side. I thought I'd pile the branches that I cut off into piles, and I proceeded to do that, only to find that at some point, I ended up totally unconscious with a gash on my skull. The question was—did I pass out and then hit my head, or did I fall and hit my head which then knocked me out?

The questions were unanswered. Nobody saw me fall, and certainly I had no recollection of it. I was unconscious for a period of time, and at some point became conscious, was able to get up, moved to my truck, and drove my truck around to the front of the church and entered the building.

My great office manager, Pastor Jennifer, saw me walking down the hall and said, "I think there's something in your hair." Then she said, "Come back please," so I came back, and she said, "Oh! You've hurt yourself! There's blood! It's bleeding on the back of your head!"

At that time, of course, there were several that responded to me to help me from our church community, including Dr. Sam, Glenn Rogers, and several others. They called an ambulance, and I was taken to the hospital, and spent basically the whole week in the hospital until late Thursday afternoon.

After all of that, I discovered when I went back over the video footage of our security cameras at the church, it appears that I simply tripped over a branch walking backwards, and ended up completely on my back on the parking lot. As I fell, my head can be seen bouncing off the parking lot and coming to rest and ultimately me becoming unconscious.

All that to say this—life is short, and life is valuable! We never know when that's going to change for us. Spending the week in the hospital, I rested. I was uncertain as to what really happened, only finding out after being released on Thursday the footage of what happened. Up until then, the doctors and I did not know whether I had passed out because of my heart attack six years ago, or whether this was something new. We just didn't know.

I'm confident now, though, that it was simply a slip and fall accident, and I'm still here to tell a story! It could have been different. I could have been left lying out there and bled out, because no one else was present in the parking lot. No one witnessed it.

All of that again, just to say that life is so precious. It is important to make sure you live every day to the fullest! Enjoy life while you have it! It's a gift from God. I'm so thankful for those who cared for me, watched over me, and gave me the medical attention I needed.

Now I rest with three staples in my head, and otherwise basically fully recovered, and glad for it. I've got more work to do yet!

I'm sharing this with you today just because I can!

—75—
Don't Flush It!

https://www.youtube.com/watch?v=RI3ESVTED5E

I'm standing here in front of the town of Innisfil water pollution control plant on 1578 St. Johns Road in Innisfil, Ontario. This is the main water pollution control plant in town. If you're interested in knowing, it has 110 kilometers of gravity-fed sewers, along with 10 kilometers of forced mains, nine pumping stations, and they service the areas of Sandy Cove, Alcona, Belle Ewart, Friday Harbor, and Lefroy.

I've read recently that the town has had some challenges with this particular plant receiving a lot of material in the sewers that doesn't belong here. In other words, people are flushing things down their toilet that they shouldn't be, and it causes backlogs here. This causes problems for the equipment. The machinery is not intended to handle these things, and what is being flushed down the toilet is causing harm and difficulties.

So they've put together an educational program to help people understand that it's meant only for human sewage. That's the intent of the wastewater treatment plant. You can help your local wastewater facility by not flushing things down the toilet that shouldn't go down the toilet, and by putting them appropriately in their places of waste! It would actually save a lot of money in terms of repairs and operations at the water pollution plant.

As I thought about that, I thought about waste. What stuff do we put to waste flush down the toilet that really shouldn't be there? I began instantly to think of our own personal lives. Many of us flush our time down the toilet. We don't use it properly. We make waste of the time that God's given to us to use for productive purposes.

I wonder what else we flush down the toilet. What other opportunities come our way and we don't pay attention to them? We waste opportunities. God's given us all giftings. He's given us time, he's given to us resources, he's given to us mental abilities, he's given to us some skills and abilities that are meant to be shared and invested in the community, as opposed to being wasted and dumped down the toilet of life.

I'm challenging you today—make sure you're not throwing stuff down the toilet that shouldn't be there in your own personal life. Don't flush your time down the toilet. There's more important things for you to use that for. There are better places for it. I'm challenging you today to do a checklist on your own life. Are there things there that truly are being flushed down the toilet that you should be using better and for helping others?

These are some thoughts I share with you today just because I can!

—76—
Are You 'On Fire' for God?

https://www.youtube.com/watch?v=jOfAP6SM1Ps

Everybody loves a bonfire. There's something really intriguing about the formation of the flames, the heat of the flames, and the direction of the smoke. Whether it's just old branches or debris, fires are just an amazing thing to watch. They can also be useful. From time to time you have a bonfire to cook your hot dogs or marshmallows and have an evening together with friends.

I got thinking that the Bible talks about fire in a lot of ways. It talks about the eternal destiny of some people will be what's described as the "lake of fire," which is totally destructive. The fire is also very helpful imagery for the excitement—the joy and enthusiasm—that one has in terms of their faith. We talk about being "on fire" for God. I think that's really where we need to be! We need to have a flame that's so powerful inside that radiates heat, that is intriguing for others to see as we live out our faith. We need to be "on fire" for God! What better illustration is there than a bonfire? The flames burn so brightly and engage others in its environment.

I trust that your life is one of those kinds that has the "fire of God" that radiates love, and life, and warmth to all of those around you.

Just a thought for the day! And, I'm sharing it with you just because I can!

—77—
Time for a Deposit

https://www.youtube.com/watch?v=WGA30F8jC2w

Here I am at an ATM—an automatic teller machine. Who would have thought years ago that we would be walking up to a machine, putting a card in, and having money spewed out into our hands automatically? Human tellers are no longer required like they used to be—it's automatic! We just come when we need some cash, put the card in, and take our money!

Well, I got to thinking about that. I thought, "Well, maybe that's sometimes how we treat God." We just keep going to the ATM of God of heaven and asking him for help when we're in need, asking him for comfort when we lose loved ones, asking him for healing when we're sick, asking him for comfort in times when there's stress in our life, asking him for relief from the challenges we face in life, asking him for support when we feel weak, asking him to strengthen our families when there's family conflict, and asking him to help our marriages when there's marital conflict.

We're seemingly always going to him for a withdrawal from the account, but I realized long ago that you can't keep drawing out unless you do something to put it in. Unless you make some deposits, your withdrawals will end up not coming out! In a spiritual sense, I'm asking the question today, what are you putting into your relationship with God?

He's blessed you. He's helped you. He hasn't turned you down when you've called on him. He's like the ATM. But, we shouldn't treat him like an ATM! We should be investing our lives and we should be making deposits in a relationship—reading our Bible, praying, talking, communing with him, attending worship services where we can worship him and adore him—doing those kinds of things. Also, we should be helping other people, being his hands extended to them—making deposits, so to speak, into the account.

Now God, through his grace and mercy, still answers us when we pray and call on him, but how much better it is when we're in relationship with him and we've made deposits in that account? Then we can call on him with confidence, and he will hear us and answer us.

Can I challenge you today start making some more deposits in your spiritual life? It is surprising what it will do for you!

I'm sharing it with you today just because I can!

—78—
Time to Die

https://www.youtube.com/watch?v=ou8zSvVUBMY

The leaves around us are changing. It's that time of year when the beauty of fall comes, the leaves begin to change colors, and the green leaves turn often brilliantly red. Such a beautiful sight! Such a beautiful season to view our wonderful country. The interesting thing is that we think when these trees are actually showing so much life and color they're actually in the dying process!

I think we as Christians sometimes don't realize it, but our best days are when we die to ourselves—to our selfish motives and to our selfish individual desires. If we were able to die to ourselves, our lives would be so much more brilliant to other people around us. People could see the beauty of the leaves all around us. Yeah, it's a great time of year.

Let's remember that the Christian life is not about us. It's about how we can serve one another, and how we can help spread the good news that Jesus loves people. "We love one another because he first loved us." It's great to be able to be in a relationship with people where they know that they're cared for, that they're loved, and that they're embraced. That really involves us dying to ourselves, setting ourselves on the back burner, so to speak.

Interestingly enough, when you do that—when you die to yourself—they are the most rewarding moments of our lives. It is then that we feel most satisfied and fulfilled! This is because we are actually helping somebody else, encouraging somebody else, lifting them up, strengthening them, girding them up so they're strong and able to move forward. Maybe they're stuck or maybe they just need that little shove to go forward, and the words that we share make the difference!

I'm just thinking about these things today. I'm learning to die to myself so that others might live fuller and more completely.

I'm sharing this with you today just because I can!

—79—
Moving Immovable Things

https://www.youtube.com/watch?v=vvu2bmY2Z6E

We've all been watching this historic house for quite some time. It's the Wauchope House. This historic home on Innisfil Beach Road in Innisfil, Ontario, was moved to a location very close to where it is now, and put onto a foundation that was formed under it, and was ready to be left as a historic home for the community.

Since then there's been a few changes, and now they're planning to move this home up closer to the roadway. If you look really closely, there are 64 wheels underneath it, ready to move it. It's temporarily a "mobile home" of sorts! And, they're moving it.

As I thought about the Wauchope House, I thought maybe in our own individual lives there are things that we think are immovable. These are things that we would like to get out of the way, but have never believed that it's possible to move them to get them out of the way. I'm suggesting that today there are some ways that you can figure out how to move the immovable things in your life. These things might be blocking you from progress, or maybe they're the most important things in your life and you just haven't been able to push them out in front so they can be seen and beneficial to you.

I want to suggest that there are ways to move things that we really haven't thought of. Maybe it's time to think a little further—how can we move those things to where they need to be? In the end, the things that are to us immovable, if it's important to move them, I just believe that God is big enough to help us to figure out how to do it! He can help us get them out of the way, or get them out front so they can be in a place where they're fulfilling the ultimate purposes they're meant to in our lives.

These are just a few wandering thoughts today, and I'm sharing them with you just because I can!

—80—
Changing Seasons

https://www.youtube.com/watch?v=873790wBP88

It's that time of year again when we see the trees that are bare and have no leaves on them at all. It's a season of change. It's deceiving sometimes, because if we drove by and saw a tree like this with no leaves, we might assume it's dead and unproductive. We don't realize that the roots are still there and there's lots of health left in the tree. So we might think it's fruitless.

Our lives can be like this. As I thought of the parallel spiritually, I was thinking that this tree, though it looks dead, might have a lot of life yet left in it, and in its season it will produce again. In our lives, we go through seasons like that, where we seem barren, unfruitful, and unproductive. Let me encourage you—hang in there! Keep doing the right stuff! Keep fertilizing the ground, and watering your soul! Sooner or later, if you keep doing the right things, the right stuff—fruit—will follow! This may just be one of those barren seasons, but if you hold on long enough, you'll find fruit that will follow.

Let me encourage you with those words. Hang in there! Don't give up! Water your soul! Feed your soul! If you do, in the end, you will produce fruit. It's a guarantee. It's a law of sowing and reaping.

I'm sharing this with you today just because I can!

—81—
Just the Way They Are

https://www.youtube.com/watch?v=7Vx2-WVJJhE

Hey, it's that time of year again when Christmas is coming soon and people are going to be out picking out their perfect Christmas tree. They're going to be looking for a tree of a certain shape a certain size, and if it's not tall enough, or not wide enough, or not full enough, they're going to discriminate against that Christmas tree! Based on its appearance, they'll discriminate against this creation that God made—that tree that's natural, so perfect because it's natural. Somebody's going to look at it and say, "That's not the tree I want! I want a perfect tree of a particular shape and size."

And we do that to people. We look at people, and we decide whether they're going to be our friends, or how close we're going to be to them, based on their shape, their size, whether they're too tall or too short or too wide, or too heavy or too light, and we discriminate against people the same way as a Christmas tree.

You know, this tree may not be the fullest tree, but we can't live without trees like this! They produce oxygen for us, the very air we breathe in our lungs. This tree helps keep us alive! Creations like this can appear to be imperfect in our eyes because we've made a preconceived judgment call about it. This tree is perfect. It does exactly what it's supposed to do. It works in the environment to replenish the environment with oxygen. It's a piece of beauty in the midst of an ordinary person's lawn or yard. It's a wonderful tree!

I wonder if sometimes we're not careful enough, and we discriminate against people in ways that we don't even think about. We may not even be aware of our own discrimination. A tree doesn't have to be the perfect shape to be the best tree. A natural tree is the best tree. It's the way God created it. Like people. We need people of different shapes, sizes, different thoughts, different thinking patterns, different ways of functioning, tall, short, wide, or whatever else. We just need lots of different varieties, because that's how God made us! We're not just a bunch of robots that all look alike, sound alike, and think alike.

No, it's like this tree. This is a special tree. This is the perfect tree! Why? Because my grandchild planted it, and it gave me the seedling, and here it is now—it's taller than I am! It's a perfect tree. If we can begin to see the source of the creation, then maybe we can look at them differently. God is the creator. God gave those lives to us. With the creator in mind, maybe we can understand perfection differently, and say natural is best. We love people just the way they are!

I'm sharing these thoughts with you today just because I can.

—82—
You Have Intrinsic Value

https://www.youtube.com/watch?v=Gem98iPJ9IM

Today I'm looking at a piece of art. The value of the art usually depends on who the artist is. The artist creates something in their own mind, and knows what they're trying to convey, but they often leave it to the one who is observing to come up with an interpretation for themselves. But a painting is valuable because of who painted it.

When I think of that, I think of the master artist—the creator of the universe, the one who put this whole globe into orbit. Yes, the master artist is the one who created you. I meet so many people who are down on themselves and feel hopeless. They feel like they're not worthy to do stuff, they feel like they can't accomplish anything, that they're no good, and that they have no value. I want to tell you today that your value is already determined because you are a work of the master artist. You have value because you're his creation. He wants to reflect through you his glory and his workmanship. He wants others to see him in your life, because you're his creation.

I was thinking today that so many people just need to understand that you're valuable because he created you. Your life is a painting for the world to see. Your life shows what our God is really like. It shows who he is, shining forth love, compassion, care, and hope. Your life offers to this world around us something of intrinsic value. It's in you because he—the master artist—created you.

So when you're feeling down on yourself, just look in the mirror again and say, "Hey, I may not know what my life is supposed to be, or supposed to look like, but the master creator—the architect of the universe—is the one who worked on me and created me, and I'm valuable because I belong to him."

I'm sharing these thoughts with you today just because I can.

About the Author

Rev. Howard D. Courtney has been a pastor for over forty years: first as an assistant pastor at Broadway Pentecostal Church (Orangeville, Ontario, 1973–1975), then as an assistant and youth pastor at Hi-Way Pentecostal Church (Barrie, Ontario, 1975–1979), and finally as the founding pastor of Innisfil Community Church (Innisfil, Ontario, 1979–present).

When he came to pastor in Innisfil in 1979, Rev. Courtney immediately embedded himself within the fabric of the community. When the church purchased property, it was in the middle of acres of farmland, but they envisioned it as being the gateway to the town of Innisfil.

Since those early days, the Innisfil Community Church congregation has grown from a few dozen to a few hundred. The impact of the church has been significant on the community, and Rev. Courtney is recognized as an active contributor to the life of the community. The church facility is used by many community organizations. The church runs a "free" clothing store and is home to the local Innisfil Food Bank. These efforts help hundreds of vulnerable individuals and families every year.

Rev. Courtney has been the recipient of many awards and has received considerable recognition from local and national podiums, including the Queen's Golden Jubilee Medal for community service, the 125th Anniversary of Confederation of Canada Medal for community service, the Order of the Red Cross, and several others.

Engaging together with him in ministry is his hardworking and hospitable wife, Beulah, whose administrative skills were honed during a previous career as an executive assistant at the once formidable telecommunications company, Nortel Networks, in Mississauga, Ontario. Beulah has received the Caring Canadian Award, a medal from the Governor General of Canada given for "significant, sustained, or unpaid contribution to their community." Rev. Courtney's first wife, Carol, an elementary school teacher, died of cancer in 1998, and was also a great help in the life and ministry of the church.

Over the years, Rev. Courtney has held various offices within his church denomination, including Area Presbyter, and as a Member of the District Executive of the Western Ontario District of the Pentecostal Assemblies of Canada.

As exemplified by the anecdotes in this book, Rev. Courtney's theology is eminently practical. He excels in bringing spiritual insight and theological applications to everyday situations.

Innisfil Community Church and its founding pastor continue to be beacons of light to the community, bringing the hope and charity of the Christian gospel to all who might receive it.

Rev. Howard & Beulah Courtney

"The Life Center" at Innisfil Community Church

Manufactured by Amazon.ca
Bolton, ON

26122063R00098